A HISTORY OF HANDS

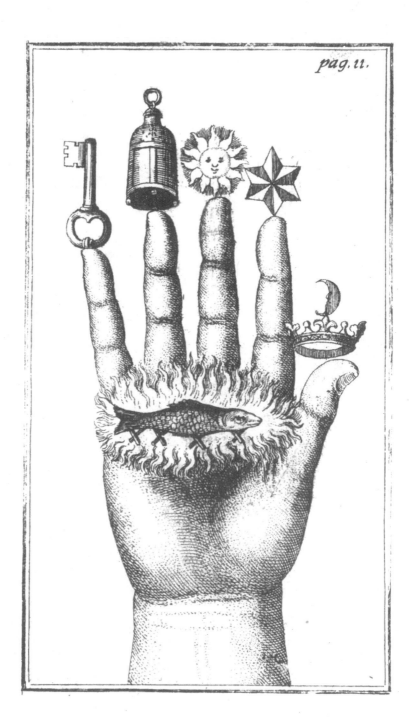

A HISTORY OF HANDS

DAVID CITINO

The Ohio State University Press
COLUMBUS

Library of Congress Cataloging-in-Publication Data

Citino, David, 1947–
A history of hands / David Citino.
p. cm.
ISBN-13: 978–0–8142–5155–3 (alk. paper)
ISBN-13: 978–0–8142–9121–4 (cd-rom)
I. Title.
PS3553.I86H57 2006
811.'6—dc22
2006021994

Cover design by Dan O'Dair.
Text design and typesetting by Jennifer Shoffey Forsythe.
Title font set in Agendia, © Ralf Herrmann, FDI font.info.
Body type set in Adobe Bembo.
Printed by Thomson-Shore, Inc.

The paper used in this publication meets the minimum
requirements of the American National Standard for Information
Sciences—Permanence of Paper for Printed Library Materials.
ANSI Z39.48-1992

9 8 7 6 5 4 3 2 1

For Mary

CONTENTS

III. New Roosevelt Sculpture Includes Wheel Chair

ACKNOWLEDGMENTS

Airfare: "A Letter to Thurber"

Antioch Review: "Death Angel, Mad Cow, Hoof & Mouth"

Connecticut Review: "Venetian Gold, Umbrian Blue"

Hotel Amerika: "Coprolites," "Real Man Strikes Out over the Phone"

Idaho Review: "No Thru Traffic," "The Retired Pastor Addresses the Tenth
   Grade Boys," "Amish Boys Busted for Buying Cocaine from Biker Gang"

Mid-American Review: "A History of Hands"

New Letters: "The Skeleton of Roaring Camp May Be a Woman"

Notre Dame Review: "Tigers Blank Tribe, 6–0," "from *Ohio Briefs:* Dad Kills
   Son in Hunting Accident," "Oldest Human Jaw Discovered"

Phi Kappa Phi Forum: "Pompeii Dream"

Poetry: "The History of Avian Abduction," "We Owe the Dead"

Poetry Northwest: "Astral Omens over the Olentangy and Scioto," "Prayer to
   the Neighbors"

Poetry Tonight: "Adam Addresses the Shop Steward"

Prairie Schooner: "Immature Red-Tail, Field Mouse in Its Talons, Delivers the
   News"

Rattle: "An Englishman Never Ventures Far without Certain Necessities"

Roanoke Review: "Controversy of the Bells"

Seneca Review: "In the Taxidermy Shop"

Shenandoah: "Penguins in Trouble Worldwide"

Smartish Pace: "A Brief History of Migration Disasters"

Southern Humanities Review: "Leadbelly Plays Severance Hall, and I Become
   a Folk Singer," "Ladders"

Southern Review: "New Roosevelt Sculpture Includes Wheel Chair," "Scien-
   tists Claim Fish Feel Pain," "Sclerosis Poem," "The River of Sclerosis"

Spirituality and Health: "Baby Talk, Second Grade Latin: To My Wife"

The Laurel Review: "Quod Turget, Urget," "Rocking the Casbah," "He's
   Feeling a Little Sorry"

West Branch: "Sister Mary Appassionata's Brief History of Smell"

Witness: "The Death of Gorilla Monsoon"

I. ASTRAL OMENS OVER THE OLENTANGY AND SCIOTO

ASTRAL OMENS OVER THE OLENTANGY AND SCIOTO

Everyone lives between two rivers, when
it comes down to it. As I walked out this evening,

the sky too was trying to place me, skin glowing,
scents of stars rushing in and out of my lungs,

breaths of lion, ram, water-bearer, twinned fish.
I wished to take my way down to one river

but the evening star fluttered to me, perched
on my left shoulder, its light staggering me off

toward the other, where the moon rose, where
I found you lying on your side, clothed only

in lunar light, your hip mimicking trajectories
of planets toward us and away since those first ticks

of time, apogee and perigee of woman and man
in their mortal dance. Migrant from a land older

than the stones hurtling above, you called out
to me. I knew at once you were too precious

to touch, too holy not to. Whatever we did, light
bathed us, gushed from our hands like honey,

our bones singing. We rose to see our shapes
in the grass, ageless fossils, the heavens brimming

on the river, two like minds, our bodies as close
to perfect as they'd been in a billion years.

POMPEII DREAM

He shouts out, the man
laboring above the woman.
She thinks, *He can't, he can't
hold back another moment—
I'm so damn hot.* They ride

until the ash covers his back
and she smells burning hair.
He thinks, *I'm holy stone
falling from heaven—she
burns for me alone.*

All at once, they can think
of nothing but scrubbing
their bodies with pumice
and lemon water
and leaping into the sea.

CONTROVERSY OF THE BELLS

An Italian priest vowed to hold on to his church bells despite
a court order to have them confiscated.
—*Reuters*

The priest declared he'd die before turning his music
over to the state. *Making too much noise,*
the charge. The court order, he says, is the work

of disgruntled locals who live near his Church
of the Shepherd in the old Naples neighborhood,
people so unloving the tolling keeps them stiff.

Isn't that the point? Fight the good fight, Father.
Loud as hell is sometimes good, rope, clapper,
those tones we feel deep in teeth and bone.

Toll away. Bells wake, make us pause, look up
to lights of other sites and times from wherever
we happen to be, and even if we no longer

hear the heavens of our childhood diocese,
our skies now cluttered with wires, ozone,
planes—not a damned angel in sight—

we need to be reminded of the magic music
we once expected from above our day,
as the final silence gathers in morning trees.

NO THRU TRAFFIC

The historic centers of 200 Italian districts, including Rome, Florence, Milan and Naples, were declared off-limits to cars on Sunday.
—Reuters

A century of internal combustion has dimmed
the delicate travertine, yesteryear's gesso.
Wanting to get there faster, another driver
gestures, screams at me—*Cretino! He's asking,*
I tell my children, *if your father has a pine-cone*
in his head. Fumes take the breath away.
In Rome, my sons and I lean out a window
of the *Accademia* and watch five roads
grind and groan, struggling to become one.
Salerno to Naples in morning rush, the boys
wide-eyed, gripping the seat. *Stop shouting!,*
I shout at them. In Bari, we park our rented Fiesta
on the sidewalk not far from the harbor,
negotiate with the leader of a gang of boys
to guard the car from other gangs.
This Sunday, by official decree, all going will slow
to saunter and stroll. *Buongiorno! Mi scusi,*
we'll say to neighbors, touching foreheads
as we make our way in sweet *passegiata.*
Civil citizens, we'll know no traffic but two bodies
or three abreast on pavement and stone,
arms linked, moving to cadences of the heart.

FALLING CROSS KILLS WOMAN IN
SOUTHERN ITALY

Not even Mary Magdalene—who turned
the Savior's head and sits now at his feet
could help—the name she bore eighty years.
This morning Maddalena walked the square
of Sant'Onofrio, to pray for those
she loved who might have sinned by accident.
The cross was being dug up, restored, prepared
for *festa,* coming of the *Bambino.*
Life's wait can bring us down, the light we seek
by rite and deed too much, at last, to bear.
As she had done each dawn for fifty years,
her body's work of passion, act of love,
Maddalena kissed the cross that day.

※

TIGERS BLANK TRIBE, 6–0

Still today, when we play Detroit,
   Grandfather comes back.
      The two of us sit in the glow
      of the old Philco. *Hey, Pa,* I say.
   Hey, Sonny boy. What in hell are we
coming to? Today we're putting

Bartolo Colon on the mound
   to go against Omar Olivares? When I
      was young it took some English to get
      a job on the west side, some German,
   Slovak, Slovenian, Italian.
There are no neighborhoods today,

the city all bass-ackwards. Priests
   are in jail, and the Irish get divorced.
      Czechs threw out the Slovaks.
      Russians run the Mafia.
   Still, some things don't change.
No matter how bad they are,

the Tigers always gives us fits.
   He's right. We go for
      their high heat, it's like we've
      never seen a slider, and
   of course it just won't rain.
When the game is over, Tigers

slapping asses, Colon throws
   down the rosin bag like it's on fire.
      Grandfather is gone. *So long,*
      Sonny boy, I hear, blue wisps
   of Chesterfield Kings in the room.
Goddamn it to hell, anyway.

8

QUOD TURGET, URGET

What swells, impels.
—Old medical maxim

This will be a history of swelling.
As the wise ones say, the body
knows how to urge us to act human.
A tumor big as an eggplant,

I recall an uncle bragging, months
before his end, lifting shirt to show
the scar, which made me wonder—
deep purple *melanzana* bitter

as wine vinegar—how a God
large with love and loneliness
could find so gross a way to kill.
Other loved ones had to leave,

tongues, livers, hearts grown
out of control. But there was swelling
even more compelling to a boy
studying desire. Girls twirled by,

school skirts rolled high enough
to impel the Sisters of Mercy
to brandish their rulers, try
to measure the limits of desire.

Blouses burgeoned with breasts
I imagined to be smooth as eggplants.
Radio thickened the air, longing
unspeakable, moans, sweet pleas.

All night and day, it seemed,
my pants pockets were tender, small.

I found another one who wished
to be larger. Placing our four hands

on her taut, pendulous belly,
we were enormous. We both felt it—
the gathering wave, a swelling
about to force future and past

to be delivered, to meet between us.

BABY TALK, SECOND GRADE LATIN:
TO MY WIFE

Ad Deum qui laetificat juventutem meam.
To God, the joy of my youth.
—*From the Latin Mass*

There are worlds and worlds of words
we can travel through. Where
we go enables us to say
so much greater than we've said.

We don't know at first we've changed
our grammar, become eloquent.
Latin of the acolyte,
before I knew what it meant

was the babble, coo and coo
I knew as the first words
of my native tongue, a way
to say this heavenly place

of incense, candlelight, and wine.
And you, love, gave me words
I was too young to realize
at first—hearts, lungs, lips,

and tongue—our daily intercourse
a way, day by day, to say
two lives as one, the less we two
have lost, the best words on the way.

LEADBELLY PLAYS SEVERANCE HALL, AND I BECOME A FOLK SINGER

What did you bring me?
To keep me from the gallis pole?

There was a time six strings enraptured me.
A Silvertone from Sears disfigured, scarred
my fingers for two years, until I earned,
and learned to work a classical fat neck,
and then I rose to calloused clarity
of Gibson Jumbo. I'd tremor, strum, and pluck
a heart that yearned to bleed for all the proles
who carried tools and hods under the lashes
cracked by fat-cat bosses, traitorous pols.
This music and the blood are with me still—
I hope to God they ever are—though hands
have grown sclerosis-vague, too numb to touch
the strings and frets the way they need to be.
A son plays now for me.
                              I'd tune and tune,
Lake Erie's cloud-face darkening my world
now flat, now sharp with variable winds,
fog horns moaning, ore boats riding low,
taconite ore for Cuyahoga mills.
And Cleveland, street by street, was shut up tight,
a sea of precincts segregate, sentried
against all difference. Blacks had music—
and so did whites, though they would steal the tunes
the brothers moved to, while brothers conked,
marceled their hair. "America's Great Singer
of the Folk," the *Call & Post* declared.
He came to town the year that I was born,
Cleveland, Ohio, Severance Hall, a gold,
confectionary space, home to an orchestra
thought the best in all the world by some.
He brought his friends, work-shirted, overalled,

Pete Seeger, Sonny Terry, Brownie McGhee.
That staid and sacred dust, it must have risen
from the raucous, stomping, buck-and-wing
of liberation. A modest crowd, for all its heat.
A benefit for Henry Wallace, the Progressives,
but Cleveland—all America, to tell it true—
was not progressive in 1948.
God knows it is not now. First time
that artists racially diverse would share
this stage of high-toned, European notes.
They brought the honest sweat of folk. Beats
of depot, hearth and field, of mine and heart
to which we all could dance. The pages of
the *Plain Dealer*—my route would pay
for every pick and string I'd own—noted "a crown
of white and kinky hair, singing songs
of social significance." "The Scottsboro Boys,"
"Gallis Pole," "A Pardon Song to Governor
Pat Neff," a black bard's melodies we whites
could not but hear, and hear again, duets
of each and every one. *If I had you,*
Governor Neff, like you got me, I'd wake
up in the mornin' and I'd set you free.
It's wrong to wish to sing as children do?
Backed up by fiddle, five-string banjo, harp,
we raised our voices high above the clang
of systems where the lightest few fly high,
while those different or dark too easily
go down in flames. Sometimes the simplest song
is what it takes to get the world to join.
Now this was ages—nearly one long life
ago—but your 12 shining strings still ring
inside my head, I wanted you to know,
dear Mr. Lead.

✳

SALVIA DIVINORUM: HERB OF THE GODS

One pill makes you larger, and one pill makes you small,
And the ones that mother gives you don't do anything at all.
—*Jefferson Airplane*

I'm wandering the Athens streets with friends.
      In Levis, boots, long-haired, tie-dyed, we shine
   and glitter, where just an hour before we stumbled
      dull as mud. We'd been smoking Athens County Gold,
singing union songs, the blues. A friend arrived.
      He'd scored some pills, noon-white with one blue dot.
Hog tranquilizer, acid, or the blood of Christ—
      there was conflicting testimony on Court Street.
This eucharist has moved us to that far place where
      six and twelve strings become one note, one word.
  The pretty brick of Federalist architecture
      caught in arms of ancient Appalachian ivy,
the poverty and strip mines all seem lovely now.
      I tote my Gibson in its hard-shell case, perhaps,
perhaps I left it somewhere. I'm full of myself.
      Each sound we utter comes from vatic mouths
of prophets, sages, a lake called Hope. We're wise
      as Buddha, Dylan, Lennon, the Upanishads,
Kahlil Gibran. *Om mane padme om,*
      Indeed the jewel is in the lotus, for the times
they are a-changin'. The one I walk beside
      I've known since we were egg and sperm.
We're babies now. We laugh at time, but then
      she starts to weep—because, she tells me,
squeezing my hand, *I've just come down*
      from making love to Jesus, Joan Baez
     and Jimmy Hendrix in the same white bed,
      the pill in me so holy that I'm wet beneath
my dress between my legs, my fingers, too.
      And now we know that sin is flying full of joy
  while others are forced to walk, caught

in the trip of money, credit hours, accums,
incursions into Cambodia, earthly rites
        like Christmas, Passover, the Tet offensive.
    Something I can't explain calls out my name,
        and now I want above all else to come down
from this lonely space. How could I let myself
        and those I love become this mad, this fat-
    headed, oblivious to what, who, when—
        urgencies, emergencies, the human news.
I must find out if we are still at war.

II. OWING THE DEAD

A BRIEF HISTORY OF MIGRATION DISASTERS

This wanting to go, our mortal crave,
it's enough to make us sick some days.
You can look it up. In Exodus,
tribes whining on the way from there

to there. *There went forth a wind
from the Lord*. A million quail, blown
from a migration of their own, cast
plump shadows on the sand

of the camp. The tribes ate, ate
some more, until on every dune,
retching of the wretched, a pile
of sin. His point about too much

of a good thing made, the Lord
resurrected the quail. The birds
flew up to rejoin the dance
of star and wave, music of spheres.

Ill winds can be bad news for angels
hot-rodding death or annunciation,
saviors nailed to wood or in ascension,
but birds too are blown off course.

As with humans, most crashes,
splashes of birds are the fault
of late-night joy-riding, errors
of navigation by hot-blooded young

who haven't yet been. Millions
set out over the Atlantic each fall
only to fail, blow back, splat
on sea wrack or ashore. Some

find a ship to light on, even
if it's bound another way. October,
1962. The *Mauritania* fell awash
with passerines felled by the tail

of Hurricane Daisy, swollen like
an angry God. *May the wind be
always under wing, at your back,
but—if you're hollow-boned, prone*

*to lust for lands beyond, easily
dazzled by stars, ravenous
to go from here to there at any
given time—not too hard.*

DEATH ANGEL, MAD COW, HOOF & MOUTH

The Lord ate the firstborn camels, asses,
    sons of Egypt. His death angel spewed fumes,
        smote hip and thigh. Ever ravenous for sacrifice,
Yahweh knew how to hurt a tribe, a race,

purge of primogeniture, family dirge. This
    was the start of mass murder—if you don't count
        the Flood—vicious beyond even scarlet Nile, flies.
This scriptural bloodletting and eating

meant little in my workers' neighborhood
    of sexless pets squatting on dandelion lawns.
        The cattle are lowing the poor baby wakes. But
little Lord Jesus no crying He makes.

White-hat cowboys drove their herds to market
    but they ate beans. Brave and trusty TV mounts,
        Trigger, Buttermilk, Silver, Scout battled bad guys.
Rin Tin Tin and Lassie moved me then.

But summers in Lodi, *out in the country*
    we called it, I got religion. I mowed hay, gathered
        henhouse eggs, raising raucous flutter and squawk,
filled troughs for Angus steers, nostrils

snorting steam, fat tongues feed-caked.
    I grew to know the ancient stink of covenant,
        rising gorge of belief. I was Noah, choking
in a fragrant boat. The barn, put up by Amish,

was a church that smelled like hell,
    waft of ancient waste, pies of manured straw,
        piss steaming like July rain. This was nothing
I'd known in Cleveland, though a slaughterhouse

on the west side palled August afternoons.
   Ages, we've dominioned over our herds, beasts
       bleeding our blunt hunger, lust. Now, mad cow.
Heaps of carcasses, ranks of rotting bodies

lift our sad horizons. Brain meal felled
   them, sure as any plague, our need to suck
       sweet marrow from each bone, crack of poleax
to skull, dull thud. Blood bubbling from ears,

we drop hard to our knees before
   the gleaming knives. We're rites of sacrifice,
       homicidal angels, new gods who kill and devour
even beyond hunger, vomit, then kill again.

VENETIAN GOLD, UMBRIAN BLUE

The maestros of the Quattrocento knew
ways to show how light can play on stone,
a catechism code, runes for those believers
who couldn't read, those who could.
Altar pieces, windows, walls explode: ochre,
Venetian gold, Umbrian blue. Dress is holy.
Clothes make the saint, what tells *who.*
Naked winged one, lion, eagle, ox? Evangelist.
A girl in school-white looks through two holes,
holds a bowl of bloody eyes. Lucy. Eyes, but
no chest at all, carrying a dish, two breasts,
brown, round, warm loaves? Agatha. Jerome
groans over a fat tome, rheumy scholar, ruined eyes.
Every wheel comes with Catherine, each gridiron
puts Lawrence up in lights. Cosmas and Damian
model finery, tools of the doctor's trade. That's
Peter Apostle, keys and fish—not Peter Martyr,
head-scarved migraine throbbing through eons.
Sebastian, fatally handsome, tied to a tree, nearly
nude, writhes as arrows pierce his nipples. Here,
a mother in true virgin blue beams, moves apart
the regal baby clothes to flash a sign of what
the fuss is all about, the tiny, coral penis.
God or not, he'll always be her little man.

THE HISTORY OF AVIAN ABDUCTION

Already an ancient fireside thrill
    to chill the souls of children and holy folk
  when Herodotus heard the tales from Egypt.
     The little girl could not
        have walked up the craggy
          mountain so far
Birders, women and men, claim the greatest raptors,
    eagles, condors, can carry no more
  than their own weight, twelve pounds at most,
    from where she was
        last seen playing
          in the back yard
and though under craggy aeries far from trees,
    fossil monkey skulls in Africa are found with holes
  the size of eagle talons punched clean through,
    with her Raggedy Ann
        which too was found
          with dress in shreds
that was eons ago, when myths were not untrue,
    and a young one cursed like Ganymede
  with utter beauty could be summoned
    the body picked at
        and torn, strewn
          in brush and thorns
by a hungry eagle god with lightning eyes,
    who brought him up to paradise to serve him
  eternally in short tunic, pretty little sandals,
    the condor too full
        to fly, the eyes
          dull and satisfied.
until Hera ruined Troy because of one beautiful boy.

That is why we all, waiting for the soughing wisp and whirr
of wings of the hunter who's been tracking us all life long,
every so often, night
and day, sun, moon, rain,
look up, look up

A HISTORY OF HANDS

I. Chiapas, Mexico

A Mayan artist gives both his hands to the gods,
who use them for years to make a great mural.

The jungle, in time, rots hands, throttles
the painting, topples the palaces, buries the gods.

Now, new hands labor to bring what was to is.
At Bonampak, Chiapas state: hands hack at jungle,

scrape and claw until nine men come to life again
moments before they die again, scribes—

slaves cursed with the gift of words—crouching
at the feet of the fierce, conquering king.

In their faces we read the cost of owing
every word to the state, the gods, blood running

from hands in throes of torment as torturers
pull out fingernails with tongs glowing from

the forge. You can't expect a new king to rule
with the old hands trying to make his name.

Lips, tongues, fingers twist into obscene signs.
This raucous silence shakes the trees, leaves

like frantic hands, mad applause, waking us
from reading. One captive holds a quill in his hand,

intent upon this cautionary tale of hands, though
he weeps for those we come after, blood-chronicles

of the day, the very hour his own two hands
were cut off slowly. At dawn, new scribes

will arrive to take the pains to make new history.

2. Venezia: Santa Maria Gloriosa dei Frari

Hands appear in Western painting in the 15th century, demanding
the space between subject and seer, donor and supplicant. Mary's
white fingers struggle to keep the baby and his pudgy hands still on
her heavenly lap so Maestro Bellini's hand won't falter. Mary kneels
before Gabriel, then rises in gold and blue robes to lord it over poor
Joseph, who storms out in the middle of the night to his shop to
work alone with his hands. With steady hand, Mary parts the Bam-
bino's clothing just enough to show the world He's all man. Such
praying, scourging, angels and saints pointing the upward way, palms
waving in rows. Christ's hands are pierced and pierced, the hammer-
er's hands sinewed and gnarled, intent on doing what they need to
do. Hands cry out through the room of *Las Meninas* by Velasquez,
young ones and old, poor and rich, artist and dwarf signing to us
out of eternity. And see the stoned body lying prone on the road to
Damascus in Caravaggio's *Conversion of St. Paul,* hands held high in
a vain attempt to hold off a moment longer heaven's lightning spite,
the shadow beasts and angels we cast with our hands upon the walls
of night.

3. Cleveland, Ohio

The world reduced   to black   white
Devil or angel I can't make up   *my mind*

Ascension of Our   Lord
a new Knight of the Altar   Medieval

black cassock white surplice   clip-on tie
Latin questions   concerning
ever and ever   what a boy
wishing not to burn   aching
to make heaven   must learn to do
with   his hands

PRAYER TO THE NEIGHBORS

Scrutiny of Broad, Main or Elm,
our balance of power. The Joneses we labor
to keep up with take their duty soberly.
Neahgebur, in Old English, *near-dweller.*
Even in olden times the other was close
enough to spit. If the fires behind my eyes
weren't reflected in windows of good citizens
sentried against me, I'd run out to worry
squirrels, yowl at the moon roosting in that tree
of purple plums in the back yard, or clasp
my panting mate, our flanks bathed in sweat
of stars. *Dear near-dweller, guard*
this house and all who dwell herein
from brute acts, trash, rashness
of our nature, police blotters blooming
with felonies of broad daylight
or the night season. Regard with care
the one smiling at you over the fence—
and I swear to God I'll keep an eye on you.

ADAM ADDRESSES THE SHOP STEWARD

Work is the prime hurt, the curse
that garnishees my midnights, noons.
Not all the daydreams in the world,
erections against the work bench,
cure this. What can I hear
in the shirr and wrang of band saw?
See, through rooms of smoke, scrims
of shredded metal, cancer cells
biding their time through lymph and blood?
I'm going too soft to speak my mind.
The sweat of this factory,
women and men staining shirts
with priceless scents masked
by grease, paint thinner, linseed oil,
the pounding of a thousand time-clocks.
The rollers and horns of Joyce Mfg. Co.
ache deep in my teeth, dying miracles
of the fine bones of the hand.
My back, my feet are killing. Slowly
I'm becoming the someone I'd hate
like hell to work beside.

REAL MAN STRIKES OUT OVER THE PHONE

What are you wearing?   Chain mail. A sword and shield.
The breastplate of righteousness.

What are you wearing?   An old mother Hubbard. Granny
panties. Curlers. My best babushka.
Old flipflops.

What are you wearing?   Your mother's garter belt.
My dad's Hell's Angels T-shirt.
A Roman collar. An ID on a rope
around my neck, proof of underage.

What are you wearing?   Your sister's nipple rings.
Hickies from the lips of my best friend,
her teeth marks cool blue bruises
strewn like jewels around my throat.

What are you wearing?   Mickey Mouse ears. Tiara. Burnoose.
Chador. My burial shroud.

What are you wearing?   Nothing
but a chastity belt
forged of stainless steel,
jeans too tight to remove
over a pair of panty hose,
my thighs whispering *Goodbye.*

IN THE TAXIDERMY SHOP

Put your hands to your face,
my live, lithe one. Feathers,
beak, talons make me think
of gaudy Pleistocene beauty,

runway of the Roxy Burlesque.
Cover your bright eyes
so the world can pass you by
unannounced. I touch lips, stroke

your torso up and down ribs,
numbering every one. Barrel staves.
Earth-cave. A-frame. I won't go
to breast or thigh. There's nothing

prurient to my ministrations,
at least not yet. It's a calling,
this obsession with form.
A room fills up its space in time,

skin taut over bony scaffold,
grin of *memento mori* there
on the particle-board shelf mounted
just beyond our lives. The mind

has a way of pointing to light,
but bone knows what it knows—
skin, breath, hair—and beauty
is our guise, sight for sore eyes.

Fingers walk the Braille of days,
hemostats, eye hooks, brain spoons.
It's the mortal ache not
to leave well enough alone

on paper, in bed, in fields, in
the Hall of North American Birds,
downy owl, perfect grackle, O
my freeze-dried Cooper's hawk.

PENGUINS IN TROUBLE WORLDWIDE

—N.Y. Times

Sorrowful and joyful mysteries, they were,
those women in Medieval wimple and veil—
Olivia De Havillands, Maid Marians
but without lipstick, bouffant hairdo, padded bra,
no Errol Flynn bounding up in green tights
to titter and blush them. They kept waiting,
widows wearing his cold ring, sad beautifully.
I thought it was because our class was bad.
Second grade, I learned by heart the Latin
of the Mass, just to please them, *Ad Deum
qui laetificat, juventutem meam. I will go
unto the altar of God, Who gives joy
to my youth.* The Sisters had little joy, so
frightened did they seem of words
like *fuming, foul, forever and ever.*
Not permitted to go to the altar because
of Lot's wife, Jezebel, and Eve, they spoke
elementary theology to us children
of Ascension School. I'd do anything
not to make them cry. They broke easily,
sometimes slapped, spat at naughtiness, sass,
stamped black shoes on classroom floor.
They taught me to want to bend the knee,
not to. Now, they're disappearing
from the world, an extinction brought about
by cataclysmic climate change, seismic activity
Farewell, my teachers, fierce Sisters of Mercy.

THE RETIRED PASTOR ADDRESSES
THE TENTH GRADE BOYS

Talk is cheap, little sheep. Your ass
  is grass. The shepherd's coming back,
      nasty crook raised high. He's ready
  to sow some salt, X-ray eyes abuzz
like a billion killer bees, believe you
  me. Where will you run? What
      doth it profit a man, woman?
  You tell me, a-holes. Time after
time, time runs out. Sins
  of the father are a red flag, rag
      stuffed in the mouth of a bawling child
  as the devil is beaten out of another
little behind. It's better that a millstone
  be hanged about your necks
      and you be thrown into the sea.
  You think I'm shitting? Look
it up. Many have been drowned,
  fried for adoring wads of cash,
      gold pussy or calf. Don't low-ball
  the Lord. Holy napalm's on the way,
and you'll be grilled cheese.
  I'm talking relics charred hard,
      hooks piercing flesh, doves exploding
  in flame, saints raptured in ecstasies
of thorn. You want art? Those two,
  Homecoming king and queen,
      tail pipe clogged from the snow-bank
  they'd backed into, he staying hard
until Gabriel blows, balls glowing
  blue as the vast ocean of eternity,
      she sitting astride, pretty nipple
  a marble caught in his icy teeth,
their Chevy pointed toward forever.

SISTER MARY APPASSIONATA'S BRIEF
HISTORY OF SMELL

Lovers know the mortal sense of us. Also
morticians. In Egypt a woman in love would carry

a bag of spices *down there*—you get my drift?—
all day, gift that keeps on giving. In Merry Olde,

she'd slip a slice under her arm. *Love apple,*
a music potent enough to raise the snake.

Huysmans, panting like a dog, followed
peasant women into fields to breathe

beauty's acrid waft. Still today French whores
daub drops of love honey behind their ears

before going off to work. The apocrine glands
seep a clear fluid, scentless. Our grand impurities

lead us into temptation, bacteria blooming
on skin, lifting prints, saying our name

across the unredolent ether rifting each
from every other. After he'd preach, heal

all day in Galilean dust, believers inhaling
his humanity, the savior's flesh was heavenly.

WE OWE THE DEAD

                        this much at least, to wonder
                    what to call them. From Eve
to just this evening, more than
                        100 billion—give or take
                        some millions, depending on when

                    we start to imagine,
                shriek of Australopithecine,
murmur of Homo sapiens.
            The din swells with the *O, O*
                of each act of generation,

                        decibels of mortality, furtive
            or brazen. Some signed in,
but most left no way to say
                them. Crawling from oceans,
                    lungs filling with the bloody froth

            of moments, they lived only
        to be swept into the brine
of dissolution, their unspoken monument
        the brittle script of bones.
                Who becomes our tribal duty.

            Listen. Singing from that oak,
        from cave, river rock, fallow field,
spume of sea, the wild wind's guttural.
                Every storm and dream roars out
                    the dear names of the lost.

III. NEW ROOSEVELT
SCULPTURE
INCLUDES WHEEL CHAIR

OLDEST HUMAN JAW DISCOVERED

I.

We become museums, just in time.
A spear bites deep to touch the mushy pulp
and snake the breath away. Oldest find
from Eden's midden, dank Carpathian cave.
Your jaw, Grandfather. Five molars locked

in sockets still, ground from years lived
hand to mouth, unstubbled bone now, feast
of fire, famine-ice. Like the heart,
the jaw must labor long to keep us hot.
It comes to this, food-tools bereft

of soft. Freed from keen, pain-dumb.
Once, *Homo sapiens* arrived
from Africa to Europe, kingdom ruled
by King Neanderthal. This jaw, our own,
except it looms, huge, grinding tools

of need we'll never fathom, proof our kin
lay down with those we mock as stooping brutes,
Neanderthal, closet skeletons
no family of *Sapiens* dare speak.
The caves of genesis? Forbidden love.

What big teeth you have, Grandfather.

2.

I was a 50's child. Ohio tribe
of primitives who knew not fluoride.

Each tooth I have, baby to adult,
has failed, wracked by plaque, *cares,* probed
by X-ray, pick, clamp, MRI—

jewels of night, nothing packed tight
with mercury, amalgam, crown to root.
If I go down in flames, or drown, I'll be
the oldest poem, dental records, loss,
stumps of family tree, broken smile,

the visages of night. Priests in white
have plumbed my depths, numbered every bone.
Open wide. This shouldn't hurt a bit.
The drill-whine jerks my legs into a *danse
macabre,* my face the grimace to end all.

This ache, Grandfather. It's history.

COPROLITES

The earth and sky are full of words
       Stooping to view Jurassic strata
beneath wisps of mists
          of pleasant Gloucestershire,
   William Buckland had a hunch.
      What he knew as bezoar-stones,
          ancient fir cones, could they be
leavings of carnivore and herbivore,

extruded through intestines?
      Comparing bezoars to hyena dung—
calcium phosphate, carbonate, shards
         of bone—he learned another way,
     with bone, marble, and a name, a life
        says *I was here.* Rooting in a pile
          of Greek words, he found *coprolite*—
dung + stone. A new Adam.

The old one started it all, christening
      living things in Eden. *For whatsoever*
Adam called every living thing, that was
         the name thereof, each creature's
     calling card. *Dung beetle,* he said
       to bugs who rolled their treasures
         on the ground. *Shitepoke heron,*
he called the nervous, gangly bird

that let fly when he snuck up
     and clapped his hands. Then
he saw a thing that stopped his heart,
       a miracle beyond speaking snakes
     with hands and feet or a garden
         filled with every loveliness: fairy wings

           soft as the down on Eve's thigh,
painted with heaven's every hue,

so light that, when its wings fluttered
         Adam could read the very wind.
He touched the tiny filament of gold
            left on the leaf when the angel
   lifted off, and learned a truth,
      that beauty needs some shame,
          rises from a stain, its name.
"Butter-fly," he whispered. "Butter-fly."

LADDERS

One night, Gregor Mendel studies by candlelight
two pretty petals light as wonder, young pea flowers.

The delicacies glow in his hand like gaudy moths.
He cross-fertilizes pollen to see which seeds go green,

which yellow. Years later, Watson and Crick, like
Jacob, dream of climbing and descending, join hands

to show how, two by two, we climb the twisting ladder
all the way to what comes next. This is the way

history builds, lifts us in a passionate alphabet,
pairing of letters. A attracts T, and C seeks out G.

How do I love thee? Let me count all 64 codons.
It's the human destiny to spend what we inherit.

O, Sweet Pea, how gracefully you twist, flourish
in this arduous twining, twinning side by side, dances

of generation, steps we take to make the best selves
we can be, strewing star-stuff, egg and sperm, paying

our way, jewels of protein, whispering to each other
our genomes, *Let's climb, you and I, and pass it on.*

A LETTER TO THURBER

You rode the train to New York
from New World Columbustown,
the mild frontier, but a part
of what you were stayed put

in a fine and moral house
at the edge of home's downtown,
near the cross of Broad and High
where once men were hanged—

such news out of your past
you'd use to amuse Gothamites.
Now in that house that has survived
urban blight and then renewal,

you hear through haunted rooms
the skitter, scrabble, and creak
of brooding pigeons and writers
from noon moon until the stars go home.

The public you revolved
in the arch world of round tables,
stages, but your wit bit
like the gleaming, stone-honed edge

of a Midwest shovel. You brought
pristine Ohio light with you,
and saw well enough
to call the mostly bloodless bouts

between women and men wherever
in the world your readers were,

whether or not they found adorable
the cartoon dogs you mastered.

No misanthrope, most days, but
a decidedly unpriestly ironist
who conjures still a world free
of hypocrisy, hokum, cant.

And today, what do we give you
for the pain in, behind, the eyes,
the gathering darkness falling
like a curtain between you and us,

you and the page? Only the music
we make thinking about ourselves,
the response to antic humanity,
this laughter, remembered.

THE DEATH OF GORILLA MONSOON

Evil is almost always petty, stupid—
banal, as Hannah Arendt told us.
But then there was Gorilla Monsoon,
who knew the theatrical possibilities

of the nearly harmless side of bad—
Little Lord Tantrum kicking over
Mommy's tea roses, heirloom figurines
in front of the company.

Even my near-perfect daughter delights
in showing the world the gold ring
piercing her navel. For Gorilla,
it was the choke hold, eye gouge,

faux razor blade pulled from trunks
no tighter than the good guy's
yet a few inches more obscene,
tag-team rope wound round

and round and round the throat—
the dumb-ass ref (*Are you blind?!*)
oblivious as the villain rakes
the brave and clear matinee eyes

of Bruno Sammartino, Bobo Brazil.
What a show. Like the Roxy Burlesque
where I'd cut holy high school
to study the art of sin unfolding

high on the stage. Irma the Body,
Cupcake Cassidy and her Twin 44's.
Garter belts, cone bras, pasties,
g-string pulled aside to give a flash

of paradise, then snapped back—
and that geezer in the first row
with his binoculars. Vice on parade
up and down the runway, a crime,

ancient dance of malefactor
and voyeur. It's Gorilla Monsoon,
a real heel, or Irma the Body.
It's a daughter at fifteen saying

to the world *Watch this, I know*
you will. I'm breaking all
the laws, and we're getting
away with it, the two of us.

THE SKELETON OF ROARING CAMP
MAY BE A WOMAN

Sometimes it takes nothing less than more—
time, exposure, light—to dig beneath appearance,
slough off those secrets chaffing under the skin.
Where's the scandal in tattered cloth, seasoned bone?
When deputies discovered the century-old skeleton
in the mountains of Santa Cruz County, pistol
near the right fist, whiskey bottle lying by the left,
male duds and a $10 gold piece, they figured they had
their man. It would take a forensic anthropologist
from the university to unwrap the costume drama.
Of course some doubt remains. The little teeth of years
have gnawed away the pelvic bone that would tell us more.
But every measurement is right, and I need to believe
in heroes standing against a world of bad guys, tiny minds.
I pray, outlaw, brave evader, you drank
the bottle down, licking that last amber drop,
your toast to openness, the revelation last things
after last things bring. And now you grin
to know the world at last can grant you leave
to be no one but the better who you always knew,
truth walking up to take a good hard look.

ROCKING THE CASBAH

Art is the score, accompaniment to the very days
of us, even those most unholy. When
Operation Desert Storm kicked off—
fighters and bombers cracking open the firmament,
CNN reporters diving under hotel beds—
Armed Forces Radio started off the broadcast day
with the Clash, "Rock the Casbah," G.I.'s and fly boys—
hundreds of thousands, young and clean
as high school Spartans, Trojans, cheerleaders—
crackling with cranked-up, hot punk spunk.
"Drop your bombs between the minarets," taking
the field on holy crusade. Rock isn't art, you say?
Take poetry, which, contrary to what Auden says,
can make *everything* happen. During that same war,
Saudi poets hurled waves of formal, medieval verse
over the airwaves. Metaphors came raining
out of the sky, flaming goats, bolts of fire,
angels dumping brimstone on the sorry sons
of camels, pigs, dogs and whores. Iraqi poets
scrambled to counterattack, desert stars
shaking every night, flaming trajectories,
flowery ack-ack, flak and invective, lines broken
and bristling with hate, Patriots, killing boxes,
mobile Scuds, Phantoms, Tomahawks,
the rockets' red glare, bombs bursting in air,
the art we settle for no better than
days we break, the ways we kill.

NEW STARBUCKS OPENS IN
THE GREEN ZONE

He sips Arabian Java light,
    Paul Bremer III, ruler of Iraq,
        and says to bodyguards, *This tastes*
exactly as it does at home. They smile.

Somewhere near, an explosion.
    A thousand pounds of TNT, three tapes
        of the Qur'an, one martyr packed inside
the Toyota. There are no atheists

in the Green Zone. Belief is palpable,
    cool décor, glossolalia
        of phone, internet, video game.
A Halliburton man fluffs his beard,

types *Later,* drains the Kona Blend.
    A thousand-*dinar* lady lips and licks
        her *grande* Ethiopia decaf.
Marines check watch, weapon, GPS,

inhale their Sumatra, Zimbabwe.
    This outpost is our latest colony.
        Starbucks maintains a firm commitment to
people, communities, business.

Starbucks promotes ecological
    and economic models for the trade
        of coffee. There is nothing in the world
like a steaming cup of coffee.

AMISH BOYS BUSTED FOR BUYING
COCAINE FROM BIKER GANG

Two Old Order Amish
of Lancaster County PA, same
first and last names—but,
the paper adds, *not related*—

bought crack cocaine from
big-Harley Pagans of Philadelphia,
also bearded, but no overalls—
chains, gang colors instead.

The Amish sold it at dances
to the Antiques and Pilgrims,
Anabaptist youth groups.
It sets our wheels to turning,

gang approaching gang, shaking
hands, tribe sitting down to feast
with tribe, this love of a deal.
It's the human business

to demand whatever the supply.
That, and the duty of children,
to make the elders gray
by dreaming the unthinkable.

from *OHIO BRIEFS:* DAD KILLS SON IN HUNTING ACCIDENT

The stars above Ohio died of grief,
they dropped like leaves of oak and ash.
A father felled his son, the mortal arrow striking
deep into the breast, while they were hunting

with crossbows in rural Muskingum County.
There was so much father wanted son to know.
The horned moon moaned, closed its eyes,
it wrapped its arms about itself, while

great Orion threw his bow away, removed
his diamond belt and knelt in deep fields
of ancient dark to weep and shake for one still boy,
for all fallen prey. Cornstalks rasped a dirge,

disconsolate October winds bore the spirit
of the son from the unharvested cornfield
where the arrow laid him down, just south
of Adamsville near Rt. 93. Father had taken aim

from an open hayfield thirty yards away
when he saw stalks shiver and tick, already
a mother's hands flying to her face, shriek rising
to the clouds, father firing, thinking only, *Deer!*

SCIENTISTS CLAIM FISH FEEL PAIN

Since Father Adam, Mother Eve dropped
their lines, we've told ourselves that nothing else

can ache. August dawns, a child miles
from Cleveland—Lake Mohican—I'd thrill

to strikes of blue gill, sunfish, carp, the tug
that traveled arm to heart, bobber dragged

down under, shooting back into light,
the struggle to escape. I tried to take

the hook so gently from the mouth but made
a greater mess. If fish would swallow hook,

blood would come. I'd twist and twist the big-
eyed length of life that writhed my hand. It made

me sick. *It's just a fish!,* some older boy
sneered then, smearing morning blood across

my face. My lips, the sting, the stink, stain
of rusty lake. That day I tasted pain.

AN ENGLISHMAN NEVER VENTURES
FAR WITHOUT CERTAIN NECESSITIES

—Nor should you,

    insists the ad for British Airways. Yes,
an Englishman, like his brother the American,
Finn, Serbo-Croat, Tajik, Tutsi, Hutu and Bushman,
a man anywhere intent on collecting the finer things—
what daring and cash entitles him to, never
is far from a good book, a damn fine Scotch,
clothes that make him, leather boots, pith helmet
that screams adventure, and of course
a rapt, adoring woman, the youngest, thinnest
most flexible model available, who will stare
at him as if he were the Christ Himself
and open arms and heart, and mouth and legs
as far as she can, moaning to him *Oh*
my God!, until he's sated, unthrobbing, unerect
at last, needing only to turn over and begin
to snore as the giant bird on its way to lands
of further adventure soars and roars
through the grand, sparkling stars.

IMMATURE RED-TAIL, FIELD MOUSE IN ITS TALONS, DELIVERS THE NEWS

The hawk, black as nearly nothing
against snow-bright dawn heights,
lights on a branch above me, making
a scene framed by the window

near where I sit trying to believe
that a life made of paper, a quest
for the right arrangement of type
can save me from more appalling news.

This morning it unfolds slowly,
dark signs flapping across white:
A plane in flames plummets
to earth, passengers obedient

beneath the Please Fasten Seat Belts
sign. Father burns his little girl
with a cigar for wetting her pants.
O Daddy, she cries quietly. O Daddy.

Armies of believers clash fiercely
for reasons neither God nor Allah
understands. As with stars
and the bodies orbiting my body,

what I wish to claim as experience
depends on where I stand,
being human always a matter
of perspective and chance.

And there you have it, that's
the news, most of it bad.

The hawk can't see me, has no desire
now to look into a dwelling

merely interior, glass a problem
for birds, for humans too,
this wanting to know things
we can't even imagine.

SCLEROSIS POEM

In comedy, it's someone else who hurts.
Your tragedy, the pain's all yours,
your fate the public, stumbling *faux pas.*
The MRI affords no room to dance.
Cat's got your tongue, arms and legs jerk on,
jerk off. You start to cough, I crack
you up, shred the sponge of lung. Inflamed,
the root shoots through the tooth, skull, bathes
the brain, siren wail. You've got your nerve,
all wavering straight lines. You're a riot,
old man too soon, cerebral atrophist.
    Again this night, we'll have no sleep, no way
    of lying, acting our way out of this.

HE'S FEELING A LITTLE SORRY

> *History is what hurts.*
> —*Fredric Jameson*

No, history is what hurts us, perp with a kink
who gets off on loss, tears. Someone lovely, Mildred,
call her, loses a piece of throat, a lung, a heart
to history, which has left lipstick on ends
of her Lucky Strikes for forty years,
stained her fingers yellow with eternity.
And Robert, say, won't insist on condoms.
The pretty sailors from the bus station he
kneels to tell him no. *It kills the thrill.* Time
wastes him, years of cocktails of pretty pills.
How long it takes for history to eat
the news of every day? One life. Planes
go down like mallards full of shot.
That slum duplex turns lovely, consumed
in flame. The face of Stan at the all-night carryout
smacks the counter, spilling gum packs,
Slim Jims, blood gushing from the lens
shattered by the bullet. Those old ones
who taught me love, they suffered eons—
long nights of tumor, abscess,
sclerotic lesions, strokes, cirrhotic livers—
and were driven from the family into exile
underground, Calvary Cemetery, Holy Cross.
Some nights, when sleep can't douse the fire
in spinal cord, brain, insult of chemo
on teeth and tongue, I pore over the lights
of happiness when history nodded, messed up.
This is how we measure, treasure time, find
in fields of weed and trash the tiny flowers of joy.

NEW ROOSEVELT SCULPTURE INCLUDES
WHEEL CHAIR

The National Park Service has added a sculpture of F.D.R. in a
wheelchair at the entrance to his popular monument.
—AP

America, thanks to a conspiracy
of reporters and photogs, saw him
only from the waist up. My parents—
Guadalcanal Johnny's fervent love lines
to Mildred slashed by censors on the way
to Cleveland—weren't ready to march
up a steep slope behind a lame leader.

Mr. President, you were grand,
the Hollywood command voice, patrician
and well-heeled, but not too, the colossus
of Hyde Park and the family Philco,
outraged at the goose-stepping perfidy
of rank tyrants, *the hand that held the dagger.*
We never saw you carried from limousine

to Oval Office, from there to bed, as we
didn't see the pretty lady perched on your lap.
Before it was over, you'd set the proles
walking to work again to put shoulders
to the wheel, sent the fascists scurrying
to their bunkers. You put my parents
to bed, where they labored to make me.

The polio that sat you down is gone.
But here's another sneak attack.
Doctors are saying *M.S.* to me, reading
my lesions on the MRI. My legs move
to strange music. I grip a cane to straighten

my spine. How long before I sit
in my own chair? The doctors don't know,

but the state of Ohio labels me *Disabled,*
issues me papers stamped *H* for
Handicapped. I've been conscripted.
I won't be alone, I know. We're mobilizing,
an army ready to roll, to follow our leader
out over shining fields of the republic
to do what needs to be done.

THE RIVER OF SCLEROSIS

I stand near the confluence of two tame gods
named *Olentangy* and *Scioto,* though all day
Ohio's been swept by rain. What would I give
to be made whole again, bathe in streams that once
assured me? All rivers connect, I read somewhere.
Now I see. It's Cleveland again. The Cuyahoga twists,
going nowhere, everywhere. *Meander* was the name
of another stream that writhed through time.
You cannot step twice into the same river, Heraclitus
of Ephesus said. Still, all life long we try. I stoop
on uncertain legs made spastic by lesions

in spinal cord and brain, the mad river *Sclerosis*
miscarrying this life. I dip my hands in viscous effluent
as carp fat with tumors winnow by, the glow
of the blast furnace of U.S. Steel cupped in my palm.
An ore boat loaded low with taconite from
the Mesabi Range comes around the bend, tugs
churning up mud so vile I hear the future screams
from maternity wards of Metro General and St. John's
in my old neighborhood, gray precinct of laborers,
graves of Calvary Cemetery. Rivers break, ache us
with reflection, accept what sins we pour.

ABOUT THE COVER ILLUSTRATION

From J. H. Hollandus, artist:

This is the hand of the philosophers with their seven secret signs, to which the ancient sages [alchemists] were bound.

The thumb: Just as the thumb powerfully closes the hand, so does saltpetre do in art.

The index finger: Next to saltpetre, vitriol is the strongest salt. It penetrates all metals.

The middle finger: Sal ammoniac shines through all metals.

The ring or gold finger: Alum gleams through the metals. It has a wonderful nature and the most subtle Spiritus.

The ear finger: Common salt is the key to art.

The palm: The fish is Mercury, the fire of Sulphur . . . Beginning, middle, and end, it is the copulator, the priest who brings all things together and conjoins them.

THE
NEW YORK
WRITER'S
SOURCE
BOOK